MILK

She'll Be Comin' Round the Mountain

SIMON & SCHUSTER BOOKS FOR YOUNG READERS
Simon & Schuster Building, Rockefeller Center
1230 Avenue of the Americas, New York, New York 10020
Copyright © 1993 by Kathleen Bullock. All rights reserved including the
right of reproduction in whole or in part in any form.
SIMON & SCHUSTER BOOKS FOR YOUNG READERS
is a trademark of Simon & Schuster.
Manufactured in the United States of America

10 9 8 7 6 5 4 3 2 1

Library of Congress Cataloging-in-Publication Data
Bullock, Kathleen. She'll be comin' round the mountain / by Kathleen Bullock.
p. cm. Summary: A family welcomes a young visitor in this illustrated version of
the familiar American folk song. 1. Folk songs, English—United States—Texts.
[1. Folk songs—United States.] I. Title. PZ8.3.B89Sh 1993 811.008—dc20
92-17340 CIP ISBN: 0-671-79153-2

To the one and only Amy

She'll Be Comin' Round the Mountain

Kathleen Bullock

SIMON & SCHUSTER BOOKS FOR YOUNG READERS
Published by Simon & Schuster
New York   London   Toronto   Sydney   Tokyo   Singapore

She'll be comin' round the mountain when she comes.
She'll be comin' round the mountain when she comes.
She'll be comin' round the mountain,
She'll be comin' round the mountain,
She'll be comin' round the mountain when she comes.

She'll be drivin' six white horses when she comes.
She'll be drivin' six white horses when she comes.
She'll be drivin' six white horses,
She'll be drivin' six white horses,
She'll be drivin' six white horses when she comes.

We will all go down to meet her when she comes.
We will all go down to meet her when she comes.
We will all go down to meet her,
We will all go down to meet her,
We will all go down to meet her when she comes.

Hi Babe!

We will catch the old red rooster when she comes.
We will catch the old red rooster when she comes.
We will catch the old red rooster,
We will catch the old red rooster,
We will catch the old red rooster when she comes.

Chop!
Chop!

We will all have chicken and dumplings when she comes.
We will all have chicken and dumplings when she comes.
We will all have chicken and dumplings,
We will all have chicken and dumplings,
We will all have chicken and dumplings when she comes.

Yum!
Yum!

She will wear her red pajamas when she comes.
She will wear her red pajamas when she comes.
She will wear her red pajamas,
She will wear her red pajamas,
She will wear her red pajamas when she comes.

She will have to sleep with Grandma when she comes.
She will have to sleep with Grandma when she comes.
She will have to sleep with Grandma,
She will have to sleep with Grandma,
She will have to sleep with Grandma when she comes.

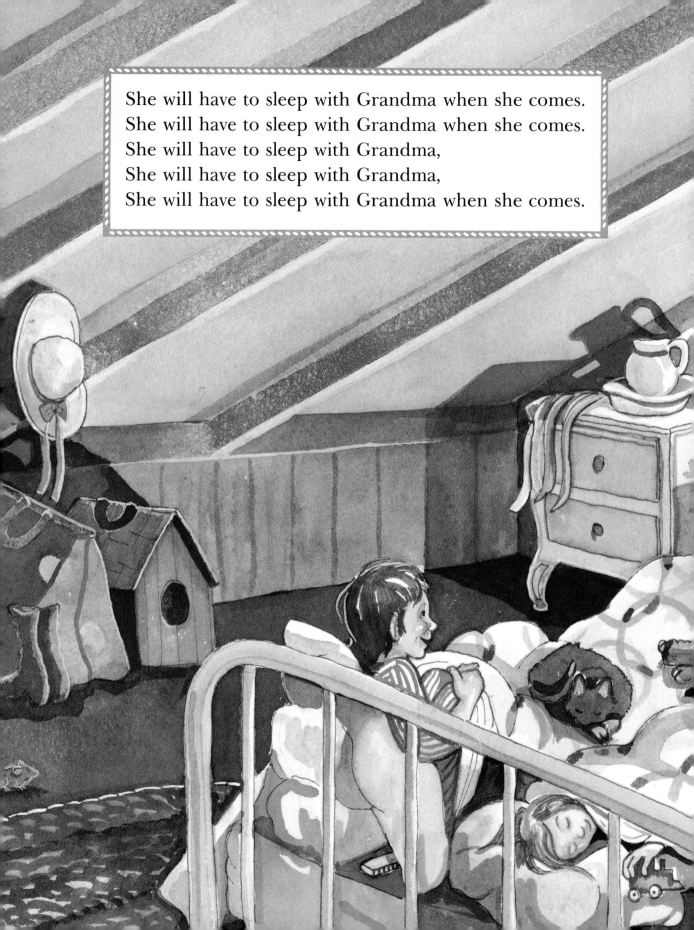

Snore! Snore!

Brightly, with spirit

1. She'll be com-in' 'round the moun-tain when she comes.____

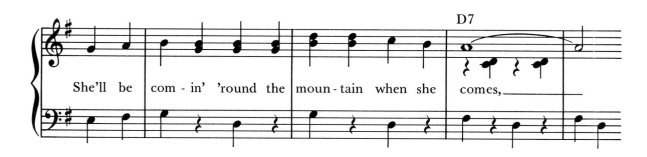

She'll be com-in' 'round the moun-tain when she comes,____

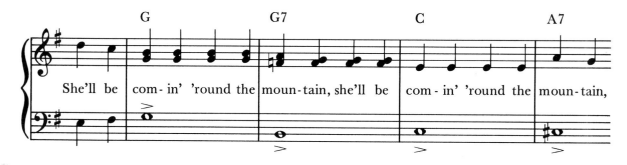

She'll be com-in' 'round the moun-tain, she'll be com-in' 'round the moun-tain,

She'll be com-in' 'round the moun-tain when she comes.____